If Nick Drake Came to My House

Ebury Press, an imprint of Ebury Publishing
One Embassy Gardens, 8 Viaduct Gdns,
Nine Elms, London SW11 7BW

Ebury Press is part of the Penguin Random House group of companies whose addresses can be found at global.penguinrandomhouse.com

Copyright © Mackenzie Crook 2024
Illustrations © Mackenzie Crook 2024

Mackenzie Crook has asserted his right to be identified as the author of this Work in accordance with the Copyright, Designs and Patents Act 1988

Penguin Random House values and supports copyright. Copyright fuels creativity, encourages diverse voices, promotes freedom of expression and supports a vibrant culture. Thank you for purchasing an authorized edition of this book and for respecting intellectual property laws by not reproducing, scanning or distributing any part of it by any means without permission. You are supporting authors and enabling Penguin Random House to continue to publish books for everyone. No part of this book may be used or reproduced in any manner for the purpose of training artificial intelligence technologies or systems. In accordance with Article 4(3) of the DSM Directive 2019/790, Penguin Random House expressly reserves this work from the text and data mining exception.

First published by Ebury Press in 2024

www.penguin.co.uk

A CIP catalogue record for this book is available from the British Library

ISBN 9781529943979

Commissioning Editor: Albert De Petrillo
Editor: Katie Fisher
Design: Loulou Clark

Printed and bound in Italy by L.E.G.O. S.p.A

Colour origination by Altaimage, London

The authorised representative in the EEA is Penguin Random House Ireland,
Morrison Chambers, 32 Nassau Street, Dublin D02 YH68.

Penguin Random House is committed to a sustainable future for our business, our readers and our planet. This book is made from Forest Stewardship Council® certified paper.

If Nick Drake Came to My House

Mackenzie Crook

EBURY
PRESS

For Jude and Scout

Foreword, with apologies to Joan Gale Thomas

In 1946 when my dad was five, he was given a book called *If Jesus Came to My House*. It imagined a little boy who opens his front door to find Jesus (also as a young boy) has come round to play.

When I was young, I would ask to see that book and was bewitched by the idea of spending an afternoon with a ghost, somebody I admired but could never really meet.

More than just meet, I'd have them to myself for a few hours, to while away some pleasant time, to chat and make friends.

This is my tribute to Joan Gale Thomas' enchanting story and illustrations, and my letter to Nick Drake, who died in 1974 when I was only three. It was another twenty years until I heard and fell in love with his music, but I often think about what I might have said to him if we'd met, and I often wish he'd been my friend.

If Nick Drake came to my house
and knocked upon the door
I'm sure I'd be more happy
than I've ever been before.

If Nick Drake came to my house
I'd like it best to be
a sunny autumn afternoon
with no one home but me.

I'd hurry down to meet him
and shake him by the hand.
I'd take his jacket from him
and hang it on the stand.

And though my mum and dad insist
that guests take off their shoes
I'd tell Nick he could leave his on
if that's what he should choose.

He'd say, "I hope you don't mind.
I brought my guitar along
and if you'd like to hear it
I could play you my new song."

I'd say, "Oh yes, I'd love to!"
and inwardly rejoice
though I know I would be grateful
just to hear his speaking voice.

But perhaps he'd like a cuppa
so I'd put the kettle on.
I'd ask him, "Sugar in your tea?"
and he'd say, "Yes please, one."

We'd take our mugs to my room
as I'm sure he'd like to see
my albums and my singles
and I'd play him an LP.

He'd close his eyes and nod along
as we sat on my bed.
I think I'd play him Elliott Smith
or maybe Radiohead.

I'd ask him how he writes his songs
and he'd be pleased to tell.
I'd ask about his tunings
and he'd explain those as well.

I'd let him read my poems
and he wouldn't laugh or sneer.
I'd tell him how his music
helped me through a troubled year.

Perhaps then I would mention
– as I hope he'd like to know –
how often now his songs are played
upon the radio.

I'd love for him to realise
how much he is admired
and the many different artists
that his music has inspired.

He'd say, "I'll play you something,"
then pick up his guitar
and perform a lilting masterpiece,
my favourite song by far.

And when the song was finished
he'd check his watch and say,
"Thanks for a lovely afternoon.
I'd best be on my way."

I'd walk him to the bus stop,
which isn't far, but first
I'd point out a house called 'Fairport'
where some friends of his rehearsed.

And when at last the bus turned up
I'd shake his hand and say,
"It was really nice to see you, Nick.
Come round another day."

I know Nick Drake can't call on me
and sing me his new tune,
and I know he'll never visit
on a sunny afternoon.

But I can play his albums
and I can recommend
Bryter Layter, Fives Leaves Left
and Pink Moon to my friends.

And I can share his records
with other people who
may not have heard those precious songs
so beautiful and few.